# Confessions of Madness
My Journey with Mental Illness

# Confessions of Madness
## My Journey with Mental Illness

by
Wendall Churchill

Single Star[*]
A Division of Ovens Onboard, Ltd.
Hilton Head Island

★

Confessions of Madness
My Journey with Mental Illness

First Published in 2019 by
Single Star
A Division of Ovens Onboard, Ltd.
Hilton Head Island

First Edition
Printed in the United States of America

For information or purchases contact:
Single Star, Publisher
PO Box 5566, Hilton Head Island, SC 29938
www.singlestar.us        sail@singlestar.us
Manufacturing by ArtBookPrinting.com
a specialty markets company of InnerWorkings, Inc.

Cover Design: Pamela Martin Ovens

Illustrations: Wendall Churchill, Italy, 1989
Instagram@wendall.churchill

Library of Congress Control Number: 2019943994
Library of Congress Cataloging-in-Publication Data

Name: Wendall Stuart Churchill
Title: Confessions of Madness, My Journey with Mental Illness
About: The emotional trauma of bipolar disorder.
ISBN 978-0-9973290-0-1 (paperback)

# Contents

# Foreword

"For me, a journey without madness would remain a fantasy, a slight whisper of light slipping into darkness. There would be no fields of glory and no cause for celebration. The image of my future was not breezy or bright, killing all my hope for a better tomorrow. If I had known the next twenty years were to be filled with misery and deep personal suffering, I could not have moved forward."

I remember clearly the first time I met Wendall. It was a Monday evening, and I was on Hilton Head Island at a NAMI Connection meeting, a support group of peers living with a mental illness. Wendall spoke about her crippling anxiety and how it took three attempts to walk through the doors and find her place amongst our group. What struck me as I listened was how she introduced herself, "I am bipolar." I also witnessed her unwillingness to claim hope and her honest, yet disturbing proclamation, "I want to die." Yet unknowingly, her actions betrayed her words as she made concrete choices to alleviate her suffering even that first evening. Over time she would uncover the kind, funny, generous, loving and creative person who already sat before us. For under layers of pain, suffering, lies and outright distortions that had oppressed her, Wendall was about to find out she was beautiful inside and out.

As I came to know Wendall I was struck by her perseverance which despite her claims could only be fueled by hope. Wendall has a quick wit and a well-developed sense of humor. The group often speaks of tools for living found in our "toolbox." Wendall feigned a lack of understanding regarding this toolbox metaphor only to come the following week with a bright, cherry red toolbox. Her wit and creativity gave us the gift of laughter that night. After the chuckling subsided Wendall asked the group to assist her in identifying her tools. What a significant moment, for in her humility she acknowledged she was no longer alone and could rely on others for help and support. Although Wendall professed to have no friends aside from her doctors and therapists, I watched as she allowed others to embrace her as she embraced them.

How grateful I am to know her embrace and you will too as your read her words. Through Wendall's memoir I find an authentic invitation to grow in understanding, empathy, and hope. Her story offers her years of holding on and the hope and healing she experiences as a result of her hard work. Wendall Churchill, is an author, artist, advocate and most appreciably, a friend.

In general, mental illness is a physical illness like diabetes which requires treatment. It is not anyone's fault. It is not a sign of weakness. Early intervention is always the best approach, because there's a chance of preventing the illness from progressing. If left untreated, at best it can destroy lives and at worst be fatal. I believe that together we can change the perception of mental illness and open doors so those suffering can walk through and find the medical attention and care that is needed to heal and recover.

If you or someone you know is struggling, you are not alone. A change in behavior or mood may be the early warning sign of a mental health condition and should never be ignored. There are many different types of mental illness and it isn't easy to simplify the range of challenges people face.

Raymond Horn, Jr.
Member, NAMI Lowcountry Board of Directors
Chairperson, NAMI Lowcountry Recovery Council

O, let me not be mad, not mad, sweet heaven!
Keep me in temper: I would not be mad!

*King Lear*
William Shakespeare

# I

## Revelation

### Charleston

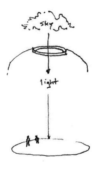

My name is Wendall, and I am mentally ill. Today I awoke in the dark alone, with only despair as my companion, and as the sun rose, the severity of my suffering only worsened despite the glory of dawn. As my erratic, psychological pathology dances dangerously close to tossing it all in, I am forced to endure yet another psychiatric hospitalization. Waking at four in the morning for the last several days has aggravated an already tortured play between wildly tumultuous highs and severe, suicidal lows. I am trapped in a fragile, broken mind, cycling between uncontrollable agitation and fits of hysterical despair, which even my fellow convalescents find a spectacle.

Despite being locked in a psychiatric facility with the reasonable anticipation of improved mental health, my anguish deepens with each passing day. Even after a dozen previous hospitalizations, I thought I might be free of the humiliation of an internal meltdown but also of the shame in self-loathing. Being back in the hospital is not only a tragic failure of self-resilience but also a severe defeat in my wish to navigate even a simple life successfully.

The chaos surrounding my nearly lifelong battle with severe mental illness has returned after only a short respite, where every day joys of simplicity were found in a quiet, undemanding, average existence. Clearly for me, a journey without madness is only a soft, simple whisper like that in a fairy tale. Being normal is no longer an option. God, help me, please...

# II

# Early Onset

## K-12

Exploding Atom

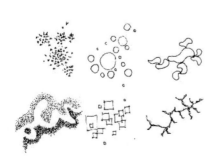

My problems began very early, for my first memory as a young child was of feeling isolated and alone, but most of all anxious, which was odd considering I was little older than a toddler. There was no abuse, but there was deep torment, internal and very real. My most vivid memory was of me as a four-year-old lying in my bed, a bed too big for a small child, looking out a sunny window and wondering why I felt so alone and ill at ease. I was aware of my isolation and unhappiness very early on, but unfortunately for me, as time passed, my trepidations only deepened. The innocent joy one might expect for a small child was lost to the angst of a tot.

Soon I was unable to handle any sort of stress, particularly when it came to school. The first day of each new grade was unbearable. I was frantic inside. Buying the pencils, new shoes, and clothing needed to last the year made my anxiety soar. I did not know how I was going to survive a day away from home, within whose walls I felt a sense of warmth and ease compared to the ominous, concrete ones of school, which for me fostered fear and anxiety versus healthy learning. The only things I enjoyed while confined in the frightening corridors of elementary education were art class and of course the half hour set aside twice a day for recess. I could doodle and imagine places of fantasy and bliss. I was a jock, so playing tag or kickball was my sixty minutes of salvation. Still, despite moments of inner quiet, I was a lonely little kid shaking from constant worry.

I insisted the family dog, Inky, sleep with me at night for I was sure feeling her warmth and presence would help soothe the pain. Yet she would abandon me within minutes, only making it that much worse. I would not go to birthday parties or even sleep over at my best friend's, only two doors down, as my nerves would not allow it. Yet above all else, the most frightening was a day of school. Even though I was gone for only a few hours, it forced me to extend myself beyond that which gave me comfort— my mother, my pets, my yard, our home. I was an emotional wreck and only ten.

Things finally reached a breaking point during fifth grade when I needed to sleep with my mother in order to survive the night. I was so nervous with worries about the following day—panicky, actually—that I was on the border of a nightly breakdown. I craved my mother's comfort, but as I grew older, she became less and less willing to hold me close. She had grown tired of my constant insecurities. Soon they sent me to a psychiatrist. I could not stand it. Being pulled out of school each week felt shameful, and clearly, I was embarrassed. Where was I going, after all? I never spoke to the psychiatrist during any of our appointments together or at least very few words were uttered. It became some sort of contest between us. I guess I won, for my parents finally let me end the agonizing year I wasted in silence after a summer of sleeping alone.

Things were not always bad, particularly during middle school. I enjoyed my athletics, since I was the star. Everybody loved me. Who wouldn't have relished that? I sure did. It felt wonderful, unlike the loneliness of my early childhood. I started to excel academically too: straight As. There were three of us who always had a 97 or 98, but of course 100 percent was better. So, we cheated and shared the various answers among us. Someone always had the answer to a question another did not know. I think the teacher knew about our mischievous behavior, but we managed to stay out of trouble. I was confident and happy. My friendships were strong and many, including a best friend, but things soon changed for the worse.

I was fourteen when my family and I moved from Chicago, the place of my birth, to a small island off the coast of South Carolina named Hilton Head. What a disaster for me. I despised it, everything about it, except of course summers on the beach. Every afternoon after *All My Children* (our favorite soap opera), we would walk down to the shore only a block away to lie in the hot summer sun and tan ourselves a golden brown. The beach was my escape, whether land sailing on the firm sand of low tide or playing paddle ball on our hand-drawn court. We had great fun and made many summer friends. Unfortunately, then came the start of the new school year.

I still did very well grade wise, but sports no

longer served my need to escape the crush of my loneliness. The only sport in the girls' athletics program that received any real attention was basketball. I was the point guard, but the coach found little about me redeeming. He believed I thought too much of myself, and that certainly was not the case. I think he just decided to dislike me because I was popular among all the teachers and was involved in all the extracurricular school activities. He helped ruin my high school experience, for he was also the dean and therefore had too much power and influence over the students' lives, whether for the good or, in my case, for the bad. The school was very sports oriented with not enough emphasis on academics. Despite my participation in the various clubs and being student-body president, I was sort of an outsider with few academic comrades. There were some very smart students I befriended, but they generally did not apply themselves. Only a few of us did. I was my class valedictorian, and embarrassingly enough I took home all but one of the awards at graduation. At least that one accolade took some attention off of me and honored someone else. It is one thing to succeed but another to command the stage at such an important moment in one's slow growth into adulthood. There, at that ceremony, in front of everyone, it turned out I was even more alone than I had thought.

# III

## The Search

### College

① reduce to form $y^2 \equiv d \pmod{p}$

(a) $3x^2 + x + 13 \equiv 0 \pmod 5$

$3 \cdot 2 \equiv 1 \pmod 5 \Rightarrow 3^{-1} = 2$

$3 \cdot 2x^2 + 2x + 2 \cdot 13 \equiv 0 \pmod 5$
$x^2 + 2x + 1 \equiv 0 \pmod 5$

inverse 2 mod 5 → 3

$(x + 2 \cdot 3)^2 + 1 - (2 \cdot 3)^2 \equiv 0 \pmod 5$
$(x + 4)^2 \equiv 3 \pmod 5$

$y^2 \equiv 3 \pmod 5$

(b) $8x^2 + 5x + 2 \equiv 0 \pmod{17}$

gcd $(8, 17) = 1$
$17 = 2 \cdot 8 + 1$     $1 = 17 - 2 \cdot 8$
$8 + 9 \cdot 1$

$\therefore 8 \cdot 8x^2 + 15(5)x + 15(2) \equiv 0 \pmod{17}$
$x^2 + 7x + 13 \equiv 0 \pmod{17}$

$9(2) \equiv 1 \pmod{17}$
$(x + 9 \cdot 7)^2 + 13 - (9 \cdot 7)^2 \equiv 0 \pmod{17}$

$\quad\quad (9 \cdot 7)^2 \cdot 13$
$\quad\quad (9 \cdot 7)^2 - 12$

$(x + 12)^2 \equiv 12 \pmod{17}$

Finally, off at college and away from home, I felt free from disappointment and positive about my future. For me, college offered the promise of professional success and hope for lasting happiness. I had a new life. I felt ready for just about anything. Life was good...as a matter of fact, it was great. During my freshman year at Middlebury (an exclusive liberal arts college in rural Vermont), I loved everything about it and participated in all the typical collegiate activities: playing intramural sports, hanging out in the local bars with friends, spending frequent weekend nights in the dorms getting high, and of course, reading books. I was so, so happy... Life could not have been better, but things changed. For despite the delight I shared with my friends and the joy of learning, I began to turn inward, thinking something must be wrong. As my studies advanced, I began to fear that my view on life with all its potential promise was not at all similar to that of my peers, since my outlook was not particularly positive or bright.

My concerns grew when I enrolled in a literature course covering the work of Walker Percy, a Southern American author whose first novel, *The Moviegoer*, won the National Book Award. It was a powerful class, inspiring deep conversations among the students in the classroom and elsewhere on campus. His books immediately piqued my interest, which I suppose was fitting with his tragic and desperate pursuit for meaning in a world corrupt with despair. Putting it simply, he writes: "AWAKE and feeling myself again, which is to say, alert, depressed-elated, and moderately terrified."[1] I thought Walker Percy was writing about me. His torment became my torment, his sense of futility in life became my internal fear of a hopeless and less compelling future. Yet we both found something temporarily with which to press on and find some weary respite in the everyday. My efforts provided only minor solace, but at least this small coup offered some temporary insight, enough to continue with my thirst for purpose in an uncertain world.

The malaise found in my collegiate years was an internal, constant void I found in a world I thought afforded me little. "The malaise is the pain of loss. The world is lost to you, the world and the people in it, and there remains only you and the world...,"[2] Percy writes. It did not matter that I was living in a pristine, surreal environment in the Green Mountains of Vermont, for nothing would have changed my pathological absorption in the loss of self. Percy repeatedly refers to what he calls "the search,"[3] a beginning point upon which one steps out of the abyss to find something that moves you, something that matters, and something to hold onto that is real. My search only caused more pain, in that I could find nothing substantive to sustain me for the long haul.

I barely survived my four years at Middlebury because my, as yet, undiagnosed illness accelerated during my senior year. My cognitive skills became cloudy as my depression worsened. It is only in retrospect that I identified my suffering as depression, but it was clear to me at the time that

17

I was very confused as evidenced by my struggle with upper-level mathematics, my major. Math had always come easily to me until drowning in it with courses titled the likes of Probability, Abstract Algebra, Real Analysis, and a thesis on Mathematical Paradoxes. It was daunting... I was totally dependent on my friend's brilliant help for all my homework (she later earned a PhD in the field). Yet, it was just the year before, during my junior year, that I had no need for help beyond that of the classroom, even though my major had by that point become significantly more difficult. During the winter term of my junior year, I was enrolled in a survey course which provided an overall exposure to the complexities of number theory. I found the class generally speaking rudimentary, yet a little exciting due to the mental calisthenics used to comprehend its full scope. Until my last year in college, my major was intriguing in a glamorous kind of way—math after all is the universal language. Senior year this all changed, as evidenced by my declining grades and my panic concerning commencement. I could not wait to graduate. Despite the fact that I finished with honors, I thought there was a real chance I might not make it. To my great relief, I did that spring, on time and as expected.

I never had a chance at being the typical college

student, brimming with infinite hope and exuberant spirit, for I had to struggle early on simply to survive the arduous days that defined much of my college life. Senior-year studies that had pained me so much and the emotional wear of my search were not the only reasons behind my unhappiness, so was the fear that my life would be beyond my capacity to manage. Almost certain that each day would not casually flow into the next like others might expect, I believed my days would be long—tragically long and difficult. These apocalyptic thoughts were not fully comprised during my college tenure, but soon thereafter I realized they had been festering for quite some time. Despite my morbid sense of anticipation, I still hoped to find moments of calm, at least enough to survive my constant discomfort.

Shortly after graduation I was invited by a friend I'd met during my senior year, a roommate of a dear classmate, to join her on a six-week trip to visit mainland China. I thought it might be the perfect opportunity to continue my quest and explore something unknown and distinctly different from my life in America. I was hoping to find something insightful, something to help in my hunt for answers to the perennial existential questions: Who am I and what purpose does my presence here serve? After all, is there any meaning in the dismal, emptiness of life?

China in the eighties was shockingly different from the culture and lifestyle I knew at home. After traveling for only a short time, it became clear that we as minorities were outsiders looking in at a world where I could not understand the concept of being antithetical to a whole population, and where what really distinguished us from them was at the very least nebulous to me at the time. Race, language, and perhaps perceived wealth were conceivably part of the answer, but not all. I suppose their isolation resulted in a mind-set in which we, the Americans, were demigods, and those few who spoke English could not wait to pull us aside to engage in lengthy discussions about life in the US and world events. Because of their overwhelming, even obsessive, interest in our lives, I felt trapped, lost in a strange world diametrically opposed to my own. Even though I was lost metaphysically at home, at least I was not a spectacle to others. All my uncertainties and concerns in the States about identity and purpose were not perceivable to those around me, and somehow that provided some solace. The identity dilemma became overwhelming in China and magnified the crisis.

# IV

## Unraveling

### Italian Summer

Imaginary Scene

After leaving China, I decided to attend the University of Virginia to complete a graduate degree in landscape architecture, an interest of mine since high school. The university was an exceptional institution for the study of any of the architectural disciplines, since Thomas Jefferson designed the heart of the campus, a pinnacle of architectural excellence. I loved my studies, but the stress of frequent late-night design charrettes wore thin. After the staggering workload of my second year, I had what most people would describe as a *nervous breakdown* during summer recess. A few of us were traveling abroad studying Italian villas of the fourteenth and fifteenth centuries in an effort to add to our credentials. We were in a foreign country with a foreign language, thus making my break from reality that much worse. The stress of overseas travel became too much for me. Actually, I should never have left the States. I was already sick, yet oblivious to the severity of the situation. My sojourn in Italy turned out to be the precipice from which I finally slipped into full-blown madness.

The search collapsed. Meaning and purpose seemed inappropriate when my emotional self disintegrated and cognitive mediocrity was itself no longer realistic. I cannot describe the horror I felt the moment I realized that my mind was crumbling, and that my capacity to function while performing even the most mundane duties of daily life was broken. I became lost in my own faltering mind. The crying, the shaking, the hysteria, were overwhelming. I clearly remember banging my head against the wall repeatedly in a Venice youth hostel when the first symptoms of the downward spiral occurred, an ill-fated attempt to quiet my internal storm. I returned home from my studies early because I had become totally dysfunctional, barely able to catch a flight back to the US. Shortly after my return, things only got worse. I did not get up in the morning, slept all day, and did not eat. It was catastrophic.

My parents decided to admit me to a psychiatric hospital in Asheville, North Carolina, because it was the nearest facility to their home on Hilton Head and came highly recommended by the psychologist who had been treating me since my tragic return from abroad. Upon first arriving at Highland, I asked what the average stay was, and it was shocking: two months plus. I refused to be admitted, and we started our drive home. Immediately my depression worsened. My father promptly turned the car around without discussion.

I was oblivious to the fact that my stay at Highland was the most therapeutic out of the many, that would follow. I saw two doctors two to three times a week each, and participated in group therapy three times plus. They kept us busy from morning to night. Months passed with no real diagnosis, except the obvious depression, despite informing my psychiatrists that there was a family history of manic depression, a genetic illness now known as bipolar disorder. Eventually they got it right, but nothing they did seemed to curb my despair or calm my agitation. Initially, I found the doctors comforting and insightful, which only partially helped me understand my emptiness and torment, yet I never really felt hopeful about finding my place in life or of having any real contentment. I knew by that point happiness was relative and was not fully obtainable, at least in my mind not for me. Despite these advancements in self-awareness, the sorrow never really eased. The search for self, with all its potential promise of hope and purpose, had failed. Nothing had really changed, except for, of course, the rapid decline of my mood.

I was eventually discharged after five months of hospitalization because the funds to continue paying for my care were by then exhausted. One month of my treatment was paid for by insurance. My parents paid for three out of pocket, and the hospital paid for the last because of their delay in treating me with the correct diagnosis. My parents spent more than one hundred thousand dollars during the fall of 1989 and could not afford more. I do not know if the doctors could have done any better in their efforts to treat my symptoms or even been able to shorten my stay, for there was a very limited number of effective medications on the market. Yet I could not possibly have imagined after all those months of professional psychiatric care that my illness would continue to deteriorate to a point beyond any external sense of personal fortitude or inner calm. I felt hopeless and with good reason, for my stay at Highland had accomplished seemingly little.

Shortly after and to my great misfortune, I was committed to Broughton Hospital, a public psychiatric facility (not a mental health country club like Highland) located in Morganton, North Carolina, for my new and relentless obsession with suicide and the consequent fixation on finding the best method for ending my life. This preoccupation was evidently concerning enough for my doctor to place me as an inpatient against my will and against my trust in the mental health system, which I was as yet blindly unaware. I knew nothing about the filth and disgrace of public psychiatric hospitals, and to my great indignation they were just like typical Hollywood portrayals: over-medicated patients aimlessly wandering the hallways; small isolation rooms with barred windows and padded cement walls; foul food that left a metallic taste in your mouth; and sex between patients often occurring throughout the day. The place was an absolute horror. I was so doped up that I did not even realize my clothing was disappearing from the few possessions I had brought with me, absconded by my roommate and others.

After initial denial and to my dismay, it was soon

apparent that involuntary commitment into a public psychiatric hospital could cause a person to behave in a fashion similar to what we might have imagined our ancestors did millennia ago. Inside that abhorrent facility, much of our behavior became consistent with those of animals. In my case, while placed in isolation for banging on the box that housed the public phone, I threw food in rebellion, scooped it up immediately, and then ate a small portion of it as if to pretend it had never really happened, thus cleaning my mess quickly in an attempt to prevent further time being locked in a room with nothing in it but a rubber mattress. The little cement cell was a disgusting and primitive place of humiliation and defeat. If I had not even attempted to act as if in a state of normality, release from the horrid room would never have happened. Despite my often good behavior outside the room among the general population, it was inevitable the staff would punish me further with additional hours in isolation. I was placed in lock down frequently for my contribution to the chaos raging on the ward. The pandemonium was a direct result of the severely mentally ill living too closely together in such a confined and unstructured environment. Even the staff was at a loss as to how to control us. My confinement did little for rectifying the situation, for there were many who aggravated things to such an extent that my behavior was considered almost routine, despite my rather bizarre reaction to the stress of commitment.

The discharge procedure was daunting. All patients had to be reviewed by a panel of six to seven doctors and nurses. They sat behind a long span of folding tables, a procedure not unlike that of a parole board hearing for the release of inmates. I was so over medicated that I was barely able to participate in the discharge process, and my freedom lay in the hands of strangers. Despite my prodigious paranoia about the staff's apparent warehouse mentality versus what should have been an empathetic yet determined effort in treating the patients with dignity and respect, I was discharged after a week of incarceration, thus surviving my own personal holocaust.

As the days and weeks passed, I realized I had little chance of escaping the life I had feared would be my future. For me, a journey without madness would remain a fantasy, a slight whisper of light slipping into darkness. There would be no fields of glory and no cause for celebration. The image of my future was not breezy or bright, killing all my hope for a better tomorrow. If I had known the next twenty years were to be filled with misery and deep personal suffering, I could not have moved forward. I would certainly have killed myself without any of the usual self-reflection or fears of regret.

# V

# Confined

## Sheppard Pratt

Despite the reality of my condition, I tried my best to move along. After taking a year off from my studies and eventually finishing graduate school by the smallest allowable margin, I secured employment in Baltimore, Maryland, but soon found almost immediately I was not truly capable of full-time work, with all its responsibilities and mental acuteness required for career success. Even with an average tenure of four years at my various places of employment, it seemed like I bounced from job to job either by being fired for excessive absenteeism or by voluntarily taking a new position at another firm in an attempt to postpone the inevitability of another termination. I must have had talent or else I would not have been employed for long by any of these firms which, as a rule, catered to high-end clientele with their exquisite tastes and deep pockets. The clients themselves knew what good design was and what was not. My bosses could have found someone else to fill my place at any time, but I guess my design skills gave me value. That is, to a point.

There were numerous hospitalizations throughout my twelve years in Baltimore, though most occurred within my first few years of living there. During my first job, which lasted three years, I was hospitalized three or four times before being fired. The following year, I was unemployed and collecting Social Security Disability benefits. I did, however, work in a grocery store part-time, but even that was tenuous and resulted in the anticipated loss of that post as well. I was out of luck and out of options, and if not for the lifesaving aid that the government provided, I would have been living on the streets, unmedicated and untreated, a danger to myself but certainly not to others. After a year of Social Security followed by eight more years of professional employment, in the end Baltimore was where everything tragically came undone: my mind, my sociability, my feelings of self worth, and my ability to simply survive the day.

Over all the years of continuous, monitored care and repeatedly being locked in mental health facilities, almost every professional who oversaw my case (at least, those following my hospitalization at Highland) made no real attempt at understanding me or my reaction to the bipolar disorder I lived with every day. There were a few that did care, though, perhaps just not enough devoted doctors who took a real interest in me as their patient or even seemed to want to address my full needs, and too few to help prevent the illness from becoming my sole companion. Not surprisingly, the few psychiatrists I found capable of treating the symptoms of my bipolar as well as my inadequate sense of self all too often seemed to lack the capacity to truly empathize with my pain. I desperately needed the help of a dedicated and compassionate physician.

I finally found such a doctor while I was an inpatient at Sheppard Pratt, a teaching hospital north of the city. I knew I had found that special psychiatrist when right from the beginning she showed a concerned and personal interest in helping me escape my torment. Perhaps because

Dr. Conlon was a resident, her commitment felt more real, more tangible. Even with the latest medical research, perhaps no doctor could expect some sort of managed care for my condition, but with her help, I thought I might find some temporary relief from my pain and maybe—if only momentarily—feel more real, more like a person, not an illness.

Upon being admitted to a psychiatric hospital, one goes through an initial interview with a psychiatrist, which was proper procedure for mental health care during and prior to my years in Baltimore. After waiting some time sitting in a very small room, Dr. Conlon finally entered, and as usual I began my rant with accelerated speech, spouting off about what would later be explained to me to be paranoia, agitation, anxiety, and severe depression. I was cognizant of being depressed, but that awareness was as far as it went. To my great surprise, she listened without judgment or languish and took great interest in deciphering my gibberish, which even to me as the patient, was nothing more than bantering about a bewildering and complex collection of irrational thoughts. I suppose she found them interesting, as she later told me that despite the disorder I had a sharp and brilliant mind. Shrinks enjoy a good challenge. I guess I was that.

Every patient needs a hero, and at the time Dr. Conlon was mine. She saved my life, for my days were filled with an exhaustive obsession with suicide. I contemplated every option possible, not wanting to fail and make my life any worse than it already was. For instance, I could not imagine how terrifying and tortuous being paralyzed after a failed attempt would be if I was consequently unable to fulfill an even greater suicidal urge from an additional stressor of that magnitude. One option that I obsessed over was hanging myself from the second-floor fire escape, but even that had unacceptable consequences. My landlord lived in the rear of the house, and I did not want to subject his little girl to seeing my hanging, lifeless body. It might have haunted her forever, and I could not bear being responsible for such a vivid and unpleasant memory. I did, however, make a very serious attempt with a large overdose of valproic acid, a well-known mood stabilizer. I took about two-and-one-half months' worth of medication, desperate to end my life and in so doing take back my self-worth and end the self-hatred. I called my doctor almost immediately after swallowing the contents of the three bottles. I guess I was afraid of dying alone. I was not, however, afraid of dying; that was clear. I just wanted to talk to her, to feel connected, if only until it began to work.

That night on the phone, she urged me to come see her at her office in Sheppard Pratt. I reluctantly went to prevent the police from showing up at my apartment and making some big scene which had already occurred many times in the past. After a brief appearance and speaking with Dr. Conlon for only a few minutes I went quietly with two security guards to the emergency room. There, they did not take me seriously, for they fed me a hamburger and left me in a room by myself for over an hour. The next thing I knew, they were trying to force activated charcoal down my throat. What god-awful stuff! It was a pasty, foul-textured-tasting liquid that would coat the intestine to block the absorption of a large overdose or an accidental poisoning of nearly any toxic chemical. Two days after my almost fatal attempt, I awoke in intensive care with my landlord standing over me; the shame became overwhelming due to the vulnerability and confusion any surviving suicide victim would feel. If I had died, my family could have sued the hospital and been awarded a large settlement for their failure to treat the mentally ill with dedicated medical attention. I did not feel relief or any sense of joy in the fact I had not succeeded, so I left the door open, perhaps indefinitely.

# VI

## Isolation

### My Thirties

During my years spent under the care of both Dr. Conlon and the doctor following her move out of state, I was in constant fear of the debilitating power of the disorder that I tragically had inherited from my mother's side of the family. If she had only known that I would be next—would she have had me? Presented with the blanket truth, my parents could have prevented a lifetime of torment and years of isolation. What a blessing it would have been! Unfortunately, that was not the case. Life was never going to be easy. I was destined to be by myself, for my illness was a painful, isolating condition that did not lend itself well to spending time with others, nor did it champion the idea of sharing one's sorrow, whether the outcome was supportive in nature or not.

I was lonely—desperately so. Living alone did not help. For me, there was no true chance at companionship where two individuals communicate as equals, since most people seemed calm and even, while I on the other hand clearly suffered so much. I withdrew and avoided participating in anything other than what was required for daily survival, whether simply going to work to earn some money or even getting out of bed to eat. I did not date. I rarely even went outside. I felt others were as uncomfortable around me as I was around them. Sensing my emotional pain, most were unable to relate to such severe mental distress. Perhaps each was fearful of the fact that they too could have been forced to fight the demons of mental instability instead of only me, whom they all found erratic and odd. Most people understood mild depression but could not even begin to fathom the full scope of my battle with insanity. I was alone and crippled by my own struggle with mental illness, while everyone else ran screaming—afraid of me.

Although, generally, I chose to be by myself out of my fear of personal rejection and worries about the transparency of my own discomfort, I did, however, have contact with a few people: one old friend from college and her extended family; an older gentleman who also suffered from depression; a friend from Highland whom I relied on extensively; a girlfriend I met at work; and most precious of all, my relationship with my cat, Charcoal, a black Persian. She was given as a gift to help comfort me shortly after my discharge from Highland. She arrived with a hole in her head from her mother's excessive grooming, and there were worries the fur might not grow back. Her hair did grow in shortly after, yet I would have loved her to death, hole or no hole. She loved me unconditionally as I did her. Her deep, loving amber eyes, her black velvety fur, and her complete devotion helped sustain me. She was a reliable, non-judging companion whom I depended on deeply. If I had not had Charcoal, I am not sure what I would have done.

On the other hand, my family could not handle me or my suffering and therefore was no support at all. My parents did not understand my pain and seemingly did not want to. It was my feeling that they did not even try. It was terribly difficult on me and left me more empty and even more alone, but even without them, in the end I at least had my doctors. They stood by me when others did not. My doctors were really the only true family I had, as pathetic as that might be. They were there when life became so difficult and tortuous that it was nearly unbearable. I saw a doctor three to four times a week, depending on how I was doing, and at one point I was regularly involved in group-therapy sessions as well. These appointments kept me functioning even if only minimally so. My doctors were true advocates with their unwavering support and undying commitment in helping me maintain even a limited sense of stability. They held vigil over my damaged but still-spirited soul, the one I so desperately needed in preventing my slip into full-blown madness. They were there when my friends and family failed me, and even when I failed myself. Without their hard work, empathy, and compassion, I would have lost my will to push forward knowing such an uncertain future lay before me.

In spite of all the treatment I received from these wonderful and caring doctors, I lost my thirties while living in Baltimore because nothing had changed. I was no better. My illness only became more severe, worsening each and every day, but then, despite my deterioration, came a very small blessing. I guess it was just dumb luck, but fortunately for me the doctor who took over my case from Dr. Conlon did not really understand proper drug therapy. He prescribed some medications be taken at levels, generally accepted by most psychiatric professionals, to be well above what is considered therapeutic (as I would later find out). Many of the drugs from my earlier treatment that he chose to continue prescribing had significant sedation as a side effect, and because of his misconceptions concerning dosage, I became completely inactive, even to the point of being comatose, which I guess was to my good fortune since my suffering was therefore limited. One particular medication he continued to prescribe was valproic acid which, as mentioned earlier, I ingested during a suicide attempt a few years prior. It had in the past produced some success in treating my bipolar, but his recommended dose resulted in a blood level so high that it left little chance of me functioning in the real world. I was severely over-medicated and slept the majority of the time. Yet it was sleep that helped comfort me from my loneliness and provided me with at least some peace, if only temporarily, from my day-to-day battle with the disorder. However, my troubles never really eased. I often slept in my clothes overnight trying to escape my suffering, not wanting to make myself any more vulnerable than I already was to the inevitable pain that would arrive early the following morning and generally devastate the entire day. I slept as many as eighteen hours a day; once I even missed a whole day of work without waking. Despite his ineptitude at ensuring a proper blood level, my doctor did succeed in providing some moments of relief and even helped me experience a minor sense of personal fortitude. Even with this therapeutic success, in the end, dreaming was the only true comfort I could find.

# VII

## Broken

### Crawling Home

After eight more years of professional employ-ment since my previous disability package, I was unable to work any longer, and again applied and was approved without fuss or bureaucrat-ic bickering. Social Security Disability Income (SSDI) was very difficult to obtain for the men-tally ill, primarily due to it hinging on a doctor's subjectivity about the severity of a diagnosis like depression with its broad spectrum of emotional distress. Nearly all applicants, even people suffer-ing with other types of ailments, were forced to face an appeals process after initially being denied; however, I was approved without one after only six months of waiting (quick by SSDI processing standards). As part of the application, I had to submit medical records, a doctor's letter explaining the details of my diagnosis, and attend a difficult and draining visit with a Social Security–appointed psychiatrist. It was exhaustive, but fortunately it worked out for me. I guess I was lucky, if that is what you want to call it.

While waiting for Social Security to decide on my case, I moved back to my mother's home in South Carolina, for I could not afford to live by myself in Baltimore any longer. Upon my return, I started seeing a psychiatrist in Charleston for medication management. Unfortunately, this involved a very long and difficult drive from Hilton Head, which made treatment very inconvenient. He did, however, have some real success in choosing the right meds to help regulate my mood, and for that I was thankful. My social worker was indispensable, for Julie helped bridge the gap between medication needs and therapeutic support. After only a year and a half of good health, it was again necessary for the doctor to experiment and find the best medication cocktail to help control my condition, since both the darkness and mania persisted. With a severe form of bipolar I disorder, my symptoms often included: depression, anxiety, agitation, irritability, paranoia, racing thoughts, mixed states, and rapid cycling. In order to treat the roller coaster and find that special cocktail, my medications were adjusted frequently, particularly the antidepressant. Many he prescribed were in a family of drugs called selective serotonin reuptake inhibitors (SSRIs) that typically produced good results for patients, but they all made the situation much worse for me. They made me severely manic and were unsuccessful at alleviating any of my depression. Those days were unbearable. Even Julie could not help.

During the terrifying hours of such a day, my mood would cycle rapidly from a dark depression coupled with acute anxiety to another extreme state, that of severe agitation mixed with explosive irritability. Then in a moment's time, it would begin all over again or, even more disabling, the two states would coexist as if there were absolutely no distinction between them. Both polar extremes were exhausting, let alone when combined. It was like drowning in the depths of a perfect storm where the ocean was black and the winds were howling, like a personal war of anguish against hysteria where misery battled insanity. Unlike Baltimore, where the darkness of depression had dominated, I could no longer escape the ugly serpent of chaos. Life was in a constant state of pandemonium, spinning out of control. Many days I could not get out of bed in the morning, and when I did, the anger and agitation made daily life unbearable. The irritability with all its manic energy could result in a quick, decisive moment where I exploded out of control at any particular annoyance, one that would have only moderately aggravated someone else. I often felt that I was a horrible person, serving society little. Killing myself seemed the best option for me and for those who were forced to deal with me whether on a daily basis or when someone at some unfortunate moment fell in my way.

Yet, despite my morbid proclivity, my desperate desire to find a better tomorrow was not yet exhausted, not yet smothered by the growing severity of the disorder. I wanted more than what I had, more than what I was given. I struggled on with a fraction of hope, regardless of everything.

# VIII

## Grotesque

### Inpatient

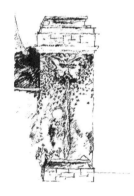

In spite of my efforts, I have failed, with my hopes now trampled, and my cries for peace silenced by defeat. I was distraught and out of control. The doctors feared for my safety, so they committed me to a mental health facility in Charleston in an attempt to control the severity of my symptoms. For me, being in a psychiatric hospital was like being housed under the pretense of successful therapeutic care and effective medical treatment. What a joke... I will never be well no matter what the doctors do. I have finally come to realize that my life will never be like that of others whose lives surely include both promise and potential. What took me so long to truly acknowledge that I was different? Decades of mental instability should have been enough, but my brief escape from the horror of my illness, felt upon first returning to my adolescent home, clearly misled me into thinking my life might flourish again as it had in the past despite all doubts to the contrary. My instincts were right; I must have been blind. My life will never be normal, never even average. I should be able to find at least a fraction of happiness in my small, little life—maybe just a tiny sliver of the bigger pie defining a world that confers upon man the innate capacity for personal delight. Yet, for me, this potential for pleasure was well beyond reach.

I am empty of joy, ugly in mind, even grotesque in nature. I am more than different; I am like an animal in a cage, wild with madness and broken in spirit. I have been forced to endure both human disgrace and public humiliation in a world where many believe mental illness is a sign of weakness and of one's own doing. We, the mentally ill, are vilified, perceived as *abnormal*, and thus, labeled with an unbearable stigma which only makes the torment worse. We have been abandoned by society, left alone in the filth of insanity. Rejection is, for me, a reality. In the end, I only have me.

Even with a life solely defined by sorrow, at least I have me. Maybe I do belong in a hospital where I am surrounded by peers; perhaps others, too, suffer as I do.

With my admission into this oppressive facility, I am thankful to at least be on an open ward solely for patients suffering with mood disorders rather than on a locked unit for the severely psychotic or on a secure hall for acute care. Almost immediately after quietly declaring my appreciation, I notice my fellow inmates are each in their own personal battle and clearly suffering in pain, but I soon realize my torment is similar to few others. Mine is black and chaotic and offers no relief. As a result of my visible agony and verbal utterances of delirium, my comrades find me strange and deviant, a spectacle of insanity beyond their own experience with mental instability. Yet despite this disparity in madness, I am their hero. I speak directly about my pain when they still have not yet found a voice. I cry in anger before they know how. From this, they find the courage to open their souls in order to confront their demons directly. Because of this unintended gift of valor, they revere me, whether I am deserving or not.

Being seen as a leader this time, as well as during many previous hospitalizations, is uplifting and an honor. They like me. They laugh *with* me not *at* me, for I suppose I am entertaining with all my outrageous outbursts and deviant antics. In the end, my fellow soldiers of misfortune leave holding me in high regard. That is more than I can say for the outside, where rejection is everywhere, including former friends and even family. I will never be normal, but will I ever belong beyond the confines of these walls, out there with real people who have real lives and have found their place in life, unlike me who has no life at all?

# IX

## The Hunt

### Lobo

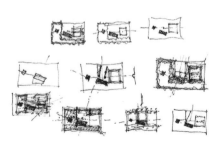

Not surprisingly, my symptoms of madness have not at all eased since being discharged. It is yet one more inpatient admission that accomplished little. The bottom line stands, for whether I am in the hospital or out in the real world, I am disenfranchised from society, left alone to continue my battle against an illness that defines—even dictates—the quality of my day. Most members of the human community wake with purpose whether for work or relaxation, while I, on the other hand, am frozen with fear at the first hint of morning light. Each day I search for my place in the world, yet fear I have none. Despite my pursuit for a modicum of salvation and moments of belonging, I remain unable to find a way through the chaos, let alone create a path to prosperity.

I cannot work; I can barely play. Crippled by my condition and unable to function like others do, I am left with the sorrow of my own professional failure. Not being able to earn my own income has been devastating and has destroyed any possibility of a positive view of my own self-worth. I assumed early on I would at least excel at something, perhaps not a hobby or social discourse, but at least at a job, a job that could provide a good living. I guess I was wrong. I have accomplished nothing. I am a failure in my own mind and a failure to others. Many say I am a poor example to the young people soon to enter the workforce, because they will need inspiration for a successful career. They must spend time with productive and energized people in order to excel, not with someone like me who must have no work ethic at all. These critics, who denounce me simply for being different, think to themselves, *she must be lazy, she must not try, or she simply succumbs to inertia. Why does she not have a family? Why does she live with her mother? What is wrong with her?* I am crazy, for god's sake. It is basic, it is simple. My mind, a bipolar mind, is ridden with faulty cells, neurons that fail me. As chemical communication breaks down, the disorder begins to rage. Order is cast aside. Soon my mind runs with excessive and disorganized speed, or it crawls in confusion, even in a daze. Today, however, I am lucid. I have focus. It is clear: I will forever be debilitated by mental illness. It is all I know; it is all I am.

I am like the legend, Lobo the Wolf, faced with adversity and stripped of dignity. His is a wrenching story, abhorrent but true. As the tale unfolds, my overwhelmed response to his plight helped clarify for me that I too am an underdog, ravaged and debilitated by a force larger than I. Lobo is only a wolf as I am only human, but each of us has been forced to battle something more powerful than either could bear, the loss of spirit from the disgrace of defeat. We are both mere mortals, whether canine or primate, each vulnerable to the deafening battle between a life of dignity or no life at all. His story is my story.

Lobo's story begins in a valley in eastern New Mexico during the late nineteenth century. His pack had become deprived of their natural prey due to a large increase in human settlement, so the wolves were forced to turn to the ranchers' livestock simply to survive. In an attempt to save their livelihoods, the ranchers tried everything but were unable to kill even one. They then hired and offered Ernest Thompson Seton, a man of historical note, an alleged bounty of one thousand dollars to kill Lobo, the alpha male, in hopes of destroying the entire pack who had thus far escaped certain death due to Lobo's brilliant cunning. Having outwitted Seton for months, Seton eventually found Lobo's weakness, a female wolf cloaked in beautiful white fur. After Lobo's spirit was trampled from losing her to Seton's insidious plan, vulnerable and weakened, he was finally caught despite his magnificent skills.

After his cruel and demoralizing capture, Lobo's resolve was destroyed and his nobility ruined. Seized and broken with no concern for himself, he lay alone, howling, his body mangled, grieving for the wolf he had hoped would be his mate. Seton had won; Lobo's spirit had lost. Like Lobo, in my narrative I too have lost for the disorder clearly has won. I too have been hunted like a wild animal by the aggressive progression of an illness, a brutal and unforgiving condition, and I now must accept that I have been condemned to a life of misfortune and pain. With my dignity shattered, the message is clear, my concerns confirmed. The door is open. Here I go...

# X

## Psychotherapy

### Dr. Rosenbaum

No, I can change. It is not yet the end, for I will do everything I can to defeat an illness, which for me, is likely fatal. I will find the help I need most, one without the limitations of a very long drive or exorbitant expense. Julie, my therapist, I love. She is good to me and takes all my calls (I am one of very few to have her private number), but because of the two-and-half-hour distance between her office and my home, *real* therapy is just not possible. It is not practical. There is only time for crisis therapy, which dominates our conversations. I see her once a month, barely enough to cope, certainly not enough to achieve any sense of real improvement in my quality of life. I need more consistency, more quality time, so I must look closer to home.

To my good fortune, after only a brief search I found a psychiatrist practicing locally, someone truly special, a doctor so committed that care for her patients is not just limited to a standard fifty-minute appointment. She gives her cell and home-phone numbers out to everyone. She is willing to talk to me seven days a week, if need-ed, which generally seems to be the case. She ac-cepts a small payment rather than her typical fee, which is well over my limited budget. She ex-tends herself beyond any doctor I have ever had. She cares. She is warm, and she is real. I need her. I have no one else.

I do have my mother and my little dog, Winston, but neither is able to ward off the extent of my loneliness nor help me cope with the everyday roller coaster of living with my condition. My mother does her best, but it is simply not enough. She lacks empathy and tender sentiment, leaving me all alone in my battle with insanity. On good days we are best of buddies, even best friends, but on the bad ones she can be horrid, showing no compassion or tangible love. This makes me suffer even more, more than I should. Yet I *do* have Dr. Rosenbaum, my newest champion. She is my sole source of comfort other than my own narrow capacity to self-soothe. She alone is capable of helping me, not because she is a competent psychiatrist but because she excels in her field.

My daily contact with her is the barometer by which not only the severity of my mood but also the depth of my loneliness are measured. I have had no one significant in my life since the onset of the disorder, other than my long list of therapists. I have been severely ill nearly half my life and have therefore missed most of its greatest rewards: marriage, children, and enduring friendships. It is my doctors that have helped fill the vacuum of my isolation. Despite my self-professed admission of feeling disconnected, meaningless, and personally destitute, at least I have had my doctors, particularly Dr. Rosenbaum. With her I feel less alone, less rejected, even special, despite my self-hatred and low self-esteem. I wonder, will anyone else enjoy me as I am? Will I ever be loved despite the illness? Will I ever love, regardless of the fear of rejection? Dr. Rosenbaum graciously accepting my daily phone calls helps ease my anxiety about my ability to connect, at least in my relationship with her. I fear I will fail with any personal affiliation for I am accustomed to seclusion, yet she stands by me to assure me I am not alone and that others too will enjoy me as she does with enthusiasm and conviction.

My raw apprehension about people and my chronic anxiety about nearly everything else cripple me and keep me from moving forward. Everything worries me. I cannot go to sleep at night without worrying about tomorrow. I have generalized anxiety disorder on top of my bipolar, and it is paralyzing. My anxiety can be so severe that I curl into a ball and lie trembling in silence in a vain attempt to smother the screaming inside. I am afraid of the unknown, which is essentially all things beyond the safety of my home and the office of my doctor. I am not agoraphobic, but it is similar if only slightly so. I do not think I would go out without the company of my mother because I might experience more stress than I can generally handle. I am lost in her absence, no matter how poorly we get along on those dark days when I am forced to suffer in silence, for with her I must be mute and not complain. Indeed, even quiet cries of pain are unwelcome. Despite her failings, if something should happen to her I would be alone, with no emotional connection to another person except for, of course, my morning conversations with my doctor.

Even my dreams offer little relief for they only re-affirm through my subconscious what the illness has done, how it has damaged even destroyed me. They are symbolic of all that has gone wrong. My dreams torment me and recur regularly, if not daily. These dreams always end the same way, no matter the variation to their nightly evolution. I often wake crying in the darkness, wondering if they will ever stop... I have dreams about being in school and no longer being able to do the work or perform at the level I expect of myself. I have dreams of good and loving friends but then end up clinging to their ghosts as they slowly vanish. I have dreams in which I am happy but wake crying, knowing life will never be the same. These themes are discussed regularly in my sessions with Dr. Rosenbaum, unlike during any of my prior decades of treatment, which were primarily crisis oriented and with the sole purpose of helping me survive the 24/7 trauma of a psychiatric disorder. In other words, real therapy did not happen until now.

Still, I am not sure the doctor and I will ever find a way for me to fully embrace my life, but maybe someday with her help, I can conquer my fears and mend my soul by seizing the damage I have suffered. I must learn to accept the weight of an illness and the pain of lost viability. Maybe that is it. Maybe that is the answer. It is this lack of acceptance of my condition, and the spoils of its wake, that limit my recovery. I am torn by the wounds of both my condition and blind denial. In order to move forward toward any real future, I must acknowledge my trauma directly and learn to welcome my future, whatever it may be. I must attend to my lesions quickly in an effort to minimize the scars of the disorder using bandages, sutures, even super glue if necessary.

It is my work with Dr. Rosenbaum that will help fix me, help repair what is broken, help glue shut the holes of insanity. Medications can only do so much. It is the therapy that holds me together. My doctor reminds me regularly that I will always suffer from mental illness, and that fact will never change. She stresses I *have* bipolar disorder and not that I *am* bipolar. She says my future is not only my illness but also how I choose to take charge of my life. I must find a cause or a hobby to help fulfill the needs of my intellect and learn to interact more confidently with others in an effort to ease the pain of seclusion. Dr. Rosenbaum is my hope, a potential lifeline to a future, but I am tired, even exhausted. Am I too worn by my suffering to seek real change? I wonder if I have the energy after all these years. Even with the help of Dr. Rosenbaum's informed guidance and unwavering commitment, I still might not make it. In spite of her advocacy, it might not be enough, but is it possible for me to succeed in my advancement? Maybe, just maybe... The obstacles are vast, potentially paralyzing, but could my exhausting, nearly life-long fight for the splendor of a real future finally prevail?

# XI

## A Beautiful Mind

### Night or Day

Today is a good day, a great day, a wonderful change from the chaos and self-deprecation. Today I feel positive, and my mind is clear. I am able to reflect upon my journey as well as the possibilities of my morrow. As I sit engrossed in thought, I begin to ponder, to ask questions, to look for answers. I think to myself, *Is my illness a curse or yet some sort of distorted blessing? Am I a better person from the trauma of mental illness? Am I more honest, more real, from years of psychotherapy?* We all live within the shadow of different grays, some darker than others, but maybe my gray, my darkness, has given me something special—something unique. Perhaps I do have something to offer, something to give. Of course, I have changed. Of course, things will be forever different from what I had hoped they would be. Yet, time has finally slowed the pace of my illness enough for me to appreciate the good in things, to see the possibilities in a new beginning. Maybe my future will be more positive than what I thought would be my fate.

After decades of trial and error, I finally have a working medication cocktail tailored specifically to me and my long list of rules (i.e., the medication cannot cause any meaningful weight gain, no tremor or uncontrollable muscle movements). The newest ingredient is lithium, an older drug that I decided to try again. I have side effects from it which I do not like, but I am by far the healthiest I have been since the onset of the disorder, so I continue with the plan. It seems senseless really, all those years wasted. There is no answer, no real reason why the lithium was not on my list sooner. I must let that thought go and welcome the stability, for it is truly incredible the difference a successful drug regimen can make to one's quality of life. It has been transformational; rather than constant suffering, today I experience moments of real joy.

Now after nearly twenty-five years of psychiatric care, I am finally able to acknowledge that I am worthy. I am beautiful. I love, and I am loved, which speaks volumes to me. Life will not always be merry. Each day will be different, whether filled with inner contentment or psychological turmoil. Every day cannot be joyful, as I have been told many times by the most helpful doctors ever in charge of my care. For me, maybe the painful days will predominate, but that is okay. I have survived my trauma, and I can breathe again.

I understand what I could not before, at least not until today. After working with Dr. Rosenbaum, I am able to see that maybe I am not so odd, not so different, but rather just a regular person walking in the real world, living life, despite all my previous fears. Even though I have felt a great sense of loss throughout the years, I have come to learn that most young people have also struggled with their own existential crisis of feeling misplaced in the world and unable to connect as part of their natural transition into adulthood. Feelings of loss and the pain of isolation are not solely unique to me, for others too, have felt adrift whether in youth or later as they matured. I, on the other hand, have always felt alone, crisis or no crisis, and things only worsened with age. *But*

I am not alone anymore. I have friends, a new knowledge of family, and even a sense of community. Now at fifty, things are different. I am no longer under the control of mental illness, for I have my health, and health is everything. Free from the grip of bipolar, maybe now I belong. Dr. Rosenbaum did that for me. She saved me from myself and reintroduced me to the world.

It is my hope that those who have suffered with years of mental illness will someday with improved health also find a little peace and, hopefully with some luck, a little happiness. It is a very different world for those who suffer, so escaping it is like a dream, a fantasy of bright lights totally obscuring the darkness. Light is everything; it is like life itself. After all my turbulent years in blackness, my journey now, though often difficult, is climbing the hills of a magnificent valley, whether on the north or the south side of the slope, whether rainy or sunny, whether winter or summer. I can make that climb... I can do it, since life has finally sprung anew.

# ACKNOWLEDGMENTS

First, I thank the professionals because they walked with me and did not abandon me on my long journey toward recovery. Indeed, there are more than a few to thank; after all, I have been at this process for a long time. I am indebted to all of you for my survival and for helping me become a healthier version of my best self. My warmest thoughts go out to: Dr. William Anixter, Maureen O'Brien, Dr. Anne Stoline, Dr. Marilyn Conlon, Dr. Randi Miller, Dr. Ricardo Fermo, Julie Lesch, and of course, Dr. Laura Rosenbaum-Bloom. Thanks to my friends for their support including: Bessie and Tom Speers, Ruth and Mac Cromwell, Karen Carroll, Pat Leonard, and Ruthie Thomas-Suh. My sincerest thanks to my mother for the laughter and a loud shout-out of appreciation to our Westie, Winston, for his compassion and empathy. His pink tongue and wagging tail have powerful healing properties unlike any p.r.n. Thanks be to Mr. Winston.

Finally, I thank my NAMI family, a local National Alliance on Mental Illness consumer support group. As part of my current routine, I see my psychiatrist and go to a NAMI meeting every Monday, so each week begins with a metal health day. It is no surprise, Monday is my favorite day of the week, for on that day I feel less ill and most notably, less alone. At NAMI, I have been able to make friends with those who also have suffered with uneven moods, distorted thoughts, and pained memories, so I am far less isolated now than I was in the past. Our meetings always begin and end with laughter. We discuss topics ranging from conquering insecurities to suicide attempts to individual therapy issues. Everyone with a psychiatric illness has the right to be there and speak their mind as they wish, as long as they stay on topic. Of course, some are more vociferous than others, me being one with a larger mouth. I have a lot to say. I do not think I bother people; rather I think they find me entertaining. I am learning who I am again. My illness robbed me of me, but through my interactions with my peers, I am re-emerging with a newfound confidence unlike ever before. I thank my NAMI friends for that and much more.

# About the Author

Wendall with her beloved dog, Winston.

Wendall Churchill moved to Hilton Head Island with her family in 1978 at age fourteen from Chicago, Illinois. She went to Sea Pines Academy for four years of upper school. She then attended Middlebury College in New England, a liberal arts college in rural Vermont. Wendall also earned a Masters in Landscape Architecture at the University of Virginia and received her degree in 1991. After working in Baltimore for many years doing high-end residential projects she later moved back to Hilton Head Island to be closer to her mother.

# NOTES

Chapter III: The Search

16    [1]**"AWAKE and feeling myself"**: Walker
       Percy, *Love in the Ruins* (Picador, 1971),
       p.353.

17    [2]**"The malaise is the pain"**: Walker Percy,
       *The Moviegoer* (Vintage Books, 1998), p.120.

17    [3]**"the search"**: Walker Percy, *The Moviegoer*
       (Vintage Books, 1998), p.11.

# Afterword

According to the National Institute of Mental Health (https://www.nimh.nih.gov), nearly one in twenty adults live with serious mental illness (SMI). SMI is defined as a mental, behavioral, or emotional disorder resulting in serious functional impairment which substantially interferes with or limits one or more major life activities. Bipolar Disorder, Major Depression, and Schizophrenia are the most prevalent SMIs.

**Concerned about suicide?** If you or someone you know is in crisis:

**Dial 911 in an emergency and ask for officers with Crisis Intervention Team (CIT) training.**

Call the toll-free **National Suicide Prevention Lifeline** (NSPL) at 1-800-273-TALK (8255), 24 hours a day, 7 days a week. The NSPL connects you with a trained crisis worker who will work to ensure that you feel safe. They will help identify options and information about mental health services in your area. Your call is confidential and free. The deaf and hard of hearing can contact the Lifeline via TTY at 1-800-799-4889.https://suicidepreventionlifeline.org/.

**How can NAMI help?**

**The National Alliance on Mental Illness** http://www.nami.org is the nation's largest grassroots mental health organization dedicated to building better lives for the millions of Americans affected by mental illness. Their helpline can be reached by calling 800-950-NAMI (6264), Monday through Friday, 10 a.m.–6 p.m., ET, or by email at info@nami.org. To learn more about these programs and other NAMI offerings, visit https://www.nami.org/

NAMI offers education programs, support groups, and other resources for individuals living with mental illness, family members, and the community. For example:

**Connection Recovery Support Group** (referenced by the author) is a peer-led support group for any adult who has experienced symptoms of a mental health condition. Participants gain insight from hearing the challenges and successes of others. The groups are led by peers, individuals living with mental illness, who've been there.

**Peer Recovery Council** is a community of people living with a mental illness committed to deepening their understanding of mental health so that they may improve the quality of their lives through education, advocacy, and service.

**Peer-to-Peer is a class for adults with mental health conditions.** The course is designed to encourage growth, healing and recovery among participants.

**In Our Own Voice** talks by individuals living with a

mental illness given to the general public to promote awareness of mental health conditions and recovery.

**Family-to-Family** is a class for families, significant others and friends of people with mental health conditions. The course is designed to facilitate a better understanding of mental health conditions, increase coping skills, and empower participants to become advocates for their family members.

**Ending the Silence** is a presentation designed for middle and high school students, school staff, and parents or guardians Audiences learn about signs and symptoms of mental health conditions, how to recognize the early warning signs, and the importance of acknowledging those warning signs.

Connect with **your** local NAMI affiliate. In Beaufort and nearby counties in South Carolina your affiliate is:

> NAMI Lowcountry (SC):
> Phone us: 843-681-2200
> Email us: nami@namilowcountry.org
> Visit us: 117 William Hilton Parkway, Suite K, Hilton Head Island, SC 29926
> Learn more about us and local offerings:
> https://namilowcountry.org/

Dick Males, President,
NAMI Lowcountry (SC) Board of Directors

# Confessions of Madness
## My Life with Mental Illness

## Colophon

The text is typeset in Adobe Caslon Pro.
For her Caslon revival, designer Carol Twombly
studied specimen pages printed by William Caslon
between 1734 & 1770. The distinction and legibility of
Caslon's type secured him the patronage of the leading
printers of his day, in England, and on the continent.
Because of its beautiful design, we agreed
that this was the perfect choice
for an artistic book.
The artwork and its layout in this book
are the work of the author Wendall Churchill.
The cover & book design are by Pamela Martin Ovens.
The publisher is Single Star on Hilton Head Island.
This book is printed in black ink on 60# white off set
paper. The cover is luxury matte lamination.
The book has been printed by
ArtBookPrinting.com a specialty markets
company of InnerWorkings, Inc. in the
United States of America.